Sam and

Story by Jenny Giles
Illustrations by Pat Reynolds

"Here is my farm,"

said Sam.

"The horse is here."

"The pig is here."

"The cow is here."

"Here comes Bingo.

No, Bingo! No!"

"Mom! Mom!

Bingo is on my farm!"

"Look, Mom.

The horse is here.

The pig is here.

The cow is here."

"The dog is here.

Look at my farm."